# 449
## Stupid Things
# Republicans
## Have Said

# 449
## Stupid Things
# Republicans
## Have Said

Ted Rueter

**Andrews McMeel
Publishing**

Kansas City

ISBN: 0-7407-4353-8

Library of Congress Control Number: 2003114759

04 05 06 07 08 VAI 10 9 8 7 6 5 4 3 2 1

## 🐘 Accounting Procedures

"In the corporate world, sometimes things aren't exactly black and white when it comes to accounting procedures."

> —George W. Bush (president, 2001–), defending actions taken by Harken Energy while he was a board member

## 🐘 Admiration

"I admired Hitler, for instance, because he came from being a little man with almost no formal education up to power."

> —Arnold Schwarzenegger (governor of California, 2003–), in a 1975 interview during the filming of a documentary, *Pumping Iron*

## 🐘 Affirmative Action

"We have not gotten into affirmative action and also Prop 54. I say we haven't gotten in that. We're having meetings about that."

> —Arnold Schwarzenegger

## 🐘 Africa

"We spent a lot of time talking about Africa, as we should. Africa is a nation that suffers from incredible disease."

—George W. Bush

## 🐘 Age

"If I had as much makeup on as he did, I'd have looked younger, too."

—Ronald Reagan (president, 1981–1989), after his 1984 presidential debate with Democratic candidate Walter Mondale

## 🐘 Aggression

"Desert Storm was a stirring victory for the forces of aggression and lawlessness."

—Dan Quayle (vice president, 1989-1993)

## 🐘 AIDS

"We're concerned about AIDS inside our White House—no mistake about it."

—George W. Bush

"Oh, you're on the side of the Sodomites? You should only get AIDS and die, you pig."

> —Michael Savage (former host of MSNBC's *Savage Nation*), to a caller. He was fired for this remark; he claimed he thought he was off the air.

## 🐘 Anecdotes

"A tax cut is really one of the anecdotes to coming out of an economic illness."

> —George W. Bush, during the 2000 presidential campaign

## 🐘 Antichrist

"You say you're supposed to be nice to the Episcopalians and the Presbyterians and the Methodists and this, that, and the other thing. Nonsense. I don't have to be nice to the spirit of the Antichrist. I can love the people who hold false opinions, but I don't have to be nice to them."

> —Pat Robertson (1988 presidential candidate), on *The 700 Club*, January 14, 1991

## 🐘 Arab Americans

"Look at who runs all the convenience stores across the country."

> —Sue Myrick (representative from North Carolina, 1995–), discussing threats to national security

## 🐘 Arms for Hostages

"We did not—repeat, did not—trade weapons or anything else for hostages, nor will we."

> —Ronald Reagan, in November 1986. In March 1987, Reagan said, "A few months ago, I told the American people I did not trade arms for hostages. My heart and my best intentions still tell me that's true, but the facts and the evidence tell me it is not."

## 🐘 Arnold

"Arnold Schwarzenegger is neither a Democrat nor a Republican. He's a Kennedy. That's why he feels so comfortable among the Kennedy men."

> —Kate O'Beirne (*National Review* magazine), commenting on Arnold Schwarzenegger's sexual exploits

## 🐘 Arrogance

"It's not your job to stop me for speeding."

> —Darrell Issa (representative from California, 2001–), to a Border Patrol police officer who stopped him for driving 90 mph through an interstate construction zone

## 🐘 Average People

"Take the average person who makes $100,000 a year. . . ."

> —Nelson Rockefeller (governor of New York, 1959–1973), beginning a lengthy discussion of economic policy

## ♟ Beauty

"I do believe you're prettier than your mama. Yes, you are, and if I was seventy years younger, I'd court you."

> —Strom Thurmond (senator from South Carolina, 1953–2002), to Chelsea Clinton, at a state dinner. At the time, Thurmond was ninety-five and Chelsea was sixteen.

## ♟ Behavior

"People sometimes do things they wouldn't do in front of their mother."

> —Barbara Cubin (representative from Wyoming, 1995–), renowned for passing around penis-shaped cookies to her male colleagues in the Wyoming state legislature

## ♟ Beliefs

"The reason I believe in a large tax cut is because it's what I believe."

> —George W. Bush

## ★ Bipartisanship

"I've lived with a Democrat for the last seventeen years. I am trained to deal with Democrats."

> —Arnold Schwarzenegger, defending his ability to work with a Democratic state legislature in California

## ★ Blacks

"So does that mean if you go into a black community, you cannot sell a gun to any black person?"

> —Barbara Cubin

"I'm not against the blacks, and a lot of the good blacks will attest to that."

> —Evan Meecham (governor of Arizona, 1987–1988)

## ★ Books

"One of the great things about books is sometimes there are some fantastic pictures."

> —George W. Bush (president, 2001–)

## 🐘 Borders

"Border relations between Canada and Mexico have never been better."

> —George W. Bush, in a press conference with the Canadian prime minister

## 🐘 Bosnia

"Bill Clinton, the man who deployed the best fighting force on the globe to build urinals in Bosnia . . ."

> —Ann Coulter (syndicated columnist and television commentator)

## 🐘 Boston

"If I were a Democrat, I suspect I'd feel a heck of a lot more comfortable in Boston than, say, America."

> —Dick Armey (representative from Texas, 1985–2002)

## 🐘 Branches of Government

"There are four departments. There's the executive, and the legislative, and the judicial—and the Bill of Rights."

> —Kenneth Wherry (senator from Nebraska, 1943–1952)

## 🐘 Briefings

"Whenever presidents say they read it, you can read that to be he was briefed."

> —Ari Fleischer (White House press secretary, 2001–2003), conceding that President Bush did not actually read a 268-page report by the Environmental Protection Agency on global warming

## 🐘 Budgets

"It's clearly a budget. It has a lot of numbers in it."

> —George W. Bush

## 🐘 Bullets

"The cost of one bullet, if the Iraqi people take it on themselves, is substantially less than that."

> —Ari Fleischer (White House press secretary, 2001–2003), suggesting the assassination of Saddam Hussein

"Let me put it this way: I had only one bullet, and I used it to shoot myself in the foot."

> —Ari Fleischer

## 🐘 George W. Bush

"The first time I met Bush 43, I knew he was different. Two things became clear. One, he didn't know very much. The other was he had the confidence to ask questions that revealed he didn't know very much."

> —Richard Perle (member, Defense Policy Board, 2001–)

"If George W. Bush is a reformer, I'm an astronaut!"

> —John McCain (senator from Arizona, 1987–), during the 2000 presidential campaign

## 🐘 Cruz Bustamante

"Cruz Bustamante is Gray Davis with a receding hairline and a mustache."

> —Arnold Schwarzenegger, during the 2003 California recall election, on the lieutenant governor of California

# 🐘 California

"Cigarettes and Botox [could soon] become the hard currency of choice. At this stage, we couldn't give California back to Mexico."

> —Ann Coulter (syndicated columnist and television commentator)

"In California, the fabulously rich support the poor with government jobs, paid for by the middle class, which is now living in Arizona."

> —Ann Coulter

# 🐘 Campaign Platform

"Say '*hasta la vista*' to Gray Davis."

> —Arnold Schwarzenegger (governor of California, 2003–)

"I can promise you that when I go to Sacramento, I will pump up Sacramento."

> —Arnold Schwarzenegger

"The public doesn't care about figures. The public cares about leadership."

> —Arnold Schwarzenegger, outlining his fiscal proposals

"Don't worry about that."

> —Arnold Schwarzenegger, detailing his
> stance on environmental protection

"Reining in government and all that other stuff."

> —Bob Dole (1996 Republican presidential
> nominee), outlining his presidential
> campaign platform

## 🐘 Campaign Staffers

"That's what happens when you get your staff from
prison work-release programs."

> —John McCain (senator from Arizona,
> 1987–), observing a food fight during the
> 2000 South Carolina Republican primary

## 🐘 Fidel Castro

"Castro couldn't even go to the bathroom unless the
Soviet Union put the nickel in the toilet."

> —Richard Nixon (president, 1969–1974), in
> September 1980

## 🐘 Celebrity

"The nice thing about being a celebrity is that when you bore people, they think it's their fault."

> —Henry Kissinger (secretary of state, 1971–1976)

## 🐘 Centuries

"That's a chapter, the last chapter of the twentieth, twentieth, the twenty-first century that most of us would rather forget. The last chapter of the twentieth century. This is the first chapter of the twenty-first century."

> —George W. Bush, on the Monica Lewinsky scandal

## 🐘 Chasing

"It's better to chase girls than boys."

> —Richard Nixon, in a newly released tape, on a controversy involving a male ambassador accused of getting drunk and fondling flight attendants

# 🐘 Christians

"I think he's a very moral man. I think he's very Christian."

> —Philip Giordano (2000 senatorial candidate from Connecticut), on his opponent, Joe Lieberman

# 🐘 Church-State Relations

"I don't believe in denominationally moving in."

> —George H. W. Bush (president, 1989–1993), during his 1984 vice presidential debate with Geraldine Ferraro, clarifying his position on church-state relations

# 🐘 Clarity

"That answer was about as clear as the Boston Harbor."

> —George H. W. Bush, to Michael Dukakis during a 1988 presidential debate

# 🐘 Bill Clinton

"He has found one of the few areas of American life that he could enter without further lowering the tone of it. And that's daytime television."

> —George F. Will (syndicated columnist and television commentator), on the prospect of Bill Clinton hosting a daytime televison talk show

"When I heard that he grew up jumping rope with the girls in his neighborhood, I knew everything I needed to know about Bill Clinton. . . . Bill Clinton couldn't credibly wear jogging shorts, and look at George Bush in that flight suit."

> —Kate O'Beirne (*National Review* magazine)

"He could talk about women who got cheated on. He could cry."

> —Roger Ailes (former Reagan media adviser, and head of the Fox News Channel), on the idea of hiring Bill Clinton to do a daytime television show

"Say what you want about the president, but his friends have convictions."

> —Dick Armey (representative from Texas, 1985–2002)

"I would rather vote for Jane Fonda than Governor Clinton. At least she has been to North Vietnam."

> —Oliver North (radio talk show host), during the 1992 presidential campaign

"We're now at the point that it's beyond whether or not this guy is a horny hick. I really think it's a question of his mental stablity. He could really be a lunatic. . . . I think it's a rational question for Americans to ask whether their president is insane."

> —Ann Coulter (syndicated columnist and television commentator)

"It's more dangerous to be a friend of Bill Clinton's than it is to be an abortionist."

> —Ann Coulter

"My biggest concern in the 107th Congress is that Bill Clinton will be with my wife in the Senate spouse's club."

> —Gordon Smith (senator from Oregon, 1997–)

## ★ Clinton-Free Zones

"Nebraska is proud of our Clinton-free air, our Clinton-free waters, and our Clinton-free morals. It will never be the same after Clinton visits here."

> —Chuck Sigerson (chairman, Nebraska Republican Party), on Bill Clinton's impending visit in December 2000. Nebraska was the fiftieth state that Clinton visited as president.

## ★ Cloning

"It would be a mistake for the United States Senate to allow any kind of human cloning to come out of that chamber."

> —George W. Bush (president, 2001–)

## 🐘 Adam Clymer

"There's Adam Clymer, major-league asshole from the *New York Times*."

> —George W. Bush to Dick Cheney during the 2000 presidential campaign, picked up by a television microphone. Cheney responded, "Big time."

## 🐘 Gary Coleman

"I'm glad that Gary Coleman lives in California. A guy like me who believes in limited government would probably have a tough time against a fellow like that, because he probably symbolizes smaller government."

> —Jeb Bush (governor of Florida, 1999–)

## 🐘 Commiserate

"I don't want nations feeling like that they can bully ourselves and our allies. I want to have a ballistic defense system so that we can make the world more peaceful, and at the same time I want to reduce our own nuclear capabilities to the level commiserate with keeping the peace."

> —George W. Bush

## 🐘 Congress

"The only difference between Congress and drunken sailors is that drunken sailors spend their own money."

> —Tom Feeney (representative from Florida, 2003–)

## 🐘 Corruption

"You scratch your back, I scratch mine. Or however you say that."

> —Suzanne Terrell (candidate for Louisiana attorney general in 2003)

## 🐘 Crime

"Obviously crime pays, or there'd be no crime."

> —G. Gordon Liddy (Watergate conspirator and radio talk show host)

## 🐘 Currencies

"I don't give a shit about the lira."

> —Richard Nixon (president, 1969–1974), in 1972, on the Italian currency

##  Tom Daschle

"I welcome you here tonight. As Senator Daschle might say, '*Bonjour.*'"

> —Tom DeLay (representative from Texas, 1985–), at a GOP event in Lancaster, Pennsylvania

"America sits and wonders why it is that al Qaeda, this ragtag bunch of terrorists scattered all over the globe, can recognize themselves. I think the difference is that al Qaeda doesn't have a Senate. Al Qaeda doesn't have a Senator Daschle."

> —Tom DeLay

##  Gray Davis

"If Gray Davis is Dr. Evil, then Cruz Bustamante is Mini-Me."

> —Sean Walsh (spokesman for California gubernatorial candidate Arnold Schwarzenegger), referring to the loathsome minion in *Austin Powers*

## 🐘 Howard Dean

"He has no appeal among Americans."

> —Ann Coulter (syndicated columnist and television commentator). She later modified her statement to say that Dean "has no appeal among 'Americana' Americans."

## 🐘 John Dean

"I wouldn't waste the twenty-five cents to buy the cartridge that would propel the bullet. . . . I despise him."

> —G. Gordon Liddy (Watergate conspirator and radio talk show host), on John Dean, counsel in the Nixon White House

## 🐘 Death Tax

"I firmly believe the death tax is good for people from all walks of life throughout our society."

> —George W. Bush (president, 2001–)

"Mr. Vice President, in all due respect, it is—I'm not sure 80 percent of the people will get the death tax. I know this: 100 percent will get it if I'm the president."

> —George W. Bush, during his third
> presidential debate with Al Gore

## 🐘 Deep Throat

"I'm not the kind of guy that is going to spend a lot of time in a garage with Bob Woodward. . . . The last time I cooperated with the *Washington Post* was in 1952, when I was a paper boy delivering the damn thing in northwest Washington."

> —Pat Buchanan (1996 presidential
> candidate), on the thirtieth anniversary of
> the Watergate break-in, denying
> speculation that he was "Deep Throat"

## 🐘 Democrats

"Democrats are for beer and girls. Republicans are for cold beer and hot girls."

> —Henry McMaster (chairman, South
> Carolina Republican Party), at a Palmetto
> Boys state leadership conference

"It's on at the same time as *Entertainment Tonight*."

> —Jeb Bush (governor of Florida, 1999–),
> explaining why he wasn't planning to
> watch the debate between his two
> Democratic opponents for governor of
> Florida in 2002

"I haven't seen a starting nine like that since the '62 Mets."

> —Dennis Miller (humorist and Republican
> political activist), on the 2004 Democratic
> presidential field

"I love these Democrats. They lose Gary Condit one day, then they pick up Marion Barry the next."

> —Bay Buchanan (political consultant)

"Democrats actually hate working-class people."

> —Ann Coulter (syndicated columnist and
> television commentator)

"The populist party of FDR, Harry Truman, and Lyndon Baines Johnson has reinvented itself as a cool hangout financed by Hollywood celebs, media yuppies, trial lawyers, multiculturalists, God haters, and the race-relations mafia, who look down on the working people who once made up the backbone of the Democratic Party."

—Laura Ingraham (radio talk show host)

"[Democrats] can't get elected unless things get worse—and things won't get worse unless they get elected."

—Jeane Kirkpatrick (ambassador to the United Nations, 1981–1985)

"Republicans believe every day is the Fourth of July, but Democrats believe every day is April 15."

—Ronald Reagan (president, 1981–1989) in 1984

##  Desire

"I didn't say I wanted the job. I said I took it."

—Christine Todd Whitman (EPA administrator, 2001–2003)

## 🐘 Thomas Dewey

"You really have to get to know Dewey to dislike him."

> —Robert Taft (senator from Ohio, 1939–1954), on Thomas Dewey, the 1948 Republican presidential nominee

## 🐘 Dictatorships

"If this were a dictatorship, it would be a heck of a lot easier—so long as I'm the dictator."

> —George W. Bush (president, 2001–)

## 🐘 Difficult Decisions

"It's the most difficult decision I've made in my entire life, except the one I made in 1978 when I decided to get a bikini wax."

> —Arnold Schwarzenegger, announcing his gubernatorial candidacy on *The Tonight Show with Jay Leno*

## 🐘 Disarmament

"I was proud the other day when both Republicans and Democrats stood with me in the Rose Garden to announce their support for a clear statement of purpose: you disarm, or we will."

—George W. Bush

## 🐘 Discrimination

"I was born in the suburbs of Boston. I was lucky to live in the northeastern United States, where . . . there is very little discrimination, or a lot less than any place else in the world."

—Mike Bloomberg (mayor of New York City, 2002–), during the 2001 campaign

"It's outrageous to think [police officers engage] in racial profiling."

—Mike Bloomberg

"Well, I'm half Jewish. Can I play nine holes?"

—Barry Goldwater (1964 presidential nominee), told by a golf course official, "Sorry, no Jews allowed"

## 🐘 Disraeli

"You read what Disraeli had to say. I don't remember what he said. He said something. He is no longer with us."

—Bob Dole (1996 presidential nominee)

## 🐘 Diversity

"Do you have blacks, too?"

—George W. Bush (president, 2001–), to Brazilian President Fernando Cardoso

## 🐘 Divine Intervention

"We ask for miracles in regard to the Supreme Court. One Justice is eighty-three years old, another has cancer, and another has a heart condition. Would it not be possible for God to put in the minds of these three judges that the time has come to retire?"

—Pat Robertson (1988 presidential candidate), launching a "prayer offensive" to remove liberal Supreme Court Justices

## 🐘 Dress Sizes

"That includes fifty-seven years of married life, six children, fourteen grandchildren, three *dress* sizes, . . . and now two presidents."

> —Barbara Bush, writing to the *Wichita Eagle* which quoted her as referring to three "breast" sizes in an earlier speech

## 🐘 Drunk Driving

"I guess that qualifies you to be president of the United States, then."

> —George Pataki (governor of New York, 1995–), after Raymond Martinez, his appointee for state DMV commissioner, admitted to a 1989 arrest for DWI

## 🐘 Dyslexia

"The woman who knew I had dyslexia—I never interviewed her."

> —George W. Bush, responding to journalist Gail Sheehey's article in *Vanity Fair*

## 🐘 Economic Ooching

"Let me tell you my thoughts about tax relief. When your economy is kind of ooching along, it's important to let people have more of their own money."

—George W. Bush

## 🐘 Education

"Sometimes when I sleep at night I think of [Dr. Seuss's] *Hop on Pop*."

—George W. Bush, in a speech on childhood education

"When I picked the secretary of education, I wanted somebody who knew something about public education."

—George W. Bush

## 🐘 Election Keys

"You can get elected by proclaiming that you are a sodomite and engage in oral sex all the time. You will get elected."

—Bob Dornan (representative from California, 1977–1996)

**Elites**

"Whenever an elite is forced to visit Middle America (Boise), he will always make sure he carries three things to ward off danger: a copy of the *Village Voice*, complete with listings of all off-Broadway productions; a battery-operated radio, tuned to NPR; and an emergency number for Tom Daschle."

> —Laura Ingraham (radio talk show host)

"This is an impressive crowd. The haves and the have-mores. Some people call you the elite. I call you my base."

> —George W. Bush, joking at the Al Smith dinner in 2000

## Embassies

"It's nothing but an eight-story microphone plugged to the Politburo."

> —Dick Armey (representative from Texas, 1985–2002), in 1987, on the U.S. embassy building in Moscow, riddled with Soviet spying devices

# 🐘 Embitterment

"I want to thank the dozens of welfare-to-work stories, the actual examples of people who made the firm and solemn commitment to work hard to embitter themselves."

    —George W. Bush (president, 2001–)

# 🐘 Endorsements

"He did support me by endorsing my opponent."

    —Damon Baldone (Louisiana state representative, 2001–), asked if the governor of Louisiana, Mike Foster, endorsed him

# 🐘 Enron

"They act like there's some billing records or some cattle scam or some fired travel aides or some blue dress."

    —Mary Matalin (aide to Vice President Cheney, 2001–2003), on Democratic criticism of the Enron scandal

## 🐘 European Americans

"I am running because there needs to be one member of Congress who stands up for the European American."

> —David Duke (candidate for Congress from Louisiana in 1999)

## 🐘 Evil

"History buffs probably noted the reunion at a Washington party a few weeks ago of three ex-presidents: Carter, Ford, and Nixon—See No Evil, Hear No Evil, and Evil."

> —Bob Dole (1996 presidential nominee), joking at the Gridiron Dinner in 1983

## 🐘 Expectations

"One of the common denominators I have found is that expectations rise above that which is expected."

> —George W. Bush

## 🐘 Extortion

"I ought to feel good. They wanted the same amount for the speaker's name as they did for mine."

> —Adam Putnam (representative from Florida, 2001–), on being a victim of an Internet extortion scheme that threatened to link congressmen's Web sites to a racist organization

## 🐘 Fabrics

"We'll be a country where the fabrics are made up of groups and loving centers."

> —George W. Bush

## 🐘 Jerry Falwell

"Every good Christian out to kick Falwell right in the ass."

> —Barry Goldwater (1964 presidential nominee)

# 🐘 Families

"Families is where our nation finds hope, where wings take dream."

—George W. Bush

"I—I will have to get into that. I mean, because, as you know, I'm very much for families. I'm very much for children and children's issues and all that stuff."

—Arnold Schwarzenegger (governor of California, 2003–), asked on the *Today* show whether he supported California's paid family leave law, the only such law in the country

"I think incest can be handled as a family matter within the family."

—Jay Dickey Jr. (representative from Arkansas, 1993–2000)

"In a weird way, Ozzy is a great antidrug promotion. Look at him and how fried his brains are from taking drugs all those years and everyone will say, 'I don't want to be like that.'"

—Dan Quayle (vice president, 1989–1993), referring to MTV rocker Ozzy Osbourne

## 🐘 Fantastic Jobs

"I want to make sure everyone in California has a great job, a fantastic job."

> —Arnold Schwarzenegger (governor of California, 2003–)

## 🐘 Farewell

"I gotta tell you, while you're all singing 'You're Gonna Miss Me While I'm Gone,' [my wife] Susan's been down in Texas singing 'It's So Miserable Without You It's Almost Like You're Here.'"

> —Dick Armey (representative from Texas, 1985–2002), at a retirement dinner

## 🐘 Father-Son Discussions

"Pussy."

> —George W. Bush (president, 2001–), at the 1988 Republican National Convention, asked by a reporter what he and his father talk about when they're not discussing politics

## 🐘 Federal Programs

"They want the federal government controlling Social Security like it's some kind of federal program."

—George W. Bush

"A billion here, a billion there: sooner it later it adds up to real money."

—Everett Dirksen (senator from Illinois, 1951–1970)

## 🐘 Feminists

"The feminist movement is just not compatible with happiness. They are not for equality; they want to kill everything masculine."

—Phyllis Schlafly (founder of the Eagle Forum), speaking to a group of college Republicans

## 🐘 Fighting Terrorism

"People say, 'How can I help on this war against terror? How can I fight evil?' You can do so by mentoring a child, by going into a shut-in's house and say 'I love you.'"

—George W. Bush

## 🐘 Finality

"I know it might put him in an awkward position that we had a discussion before finality has finally happened in this presidential race."

> —George W. Bush, describing a call to Louisiana Democratic Senator John Breaux on December 5, 2000, in which he offered Breaux a Cabinet position

## 🐘 Finding Work

"Dick Cheney and I do not want this nation to be in a recession. We want anybody who can find work to be able to find work."

> —George W. Bush

## 🐘 Fires

"Catastrophic fires burn so hot that it is incredibly hard to put them out."

> —George W. Bush, announcing his forest policy

## ![] Florida Recount

"We are bending over and taking it from the Democrats!"

> —Barbara Cubin (representative from Wyoming, 1995–), during the Florida recount battle. When some of her colleagues expressed concern about her belligerent rhetoric, she snapped, "Quiet down or you'll get a spanking."

## ![] Food Fights

"I know how hard it is for you to put food on your family."

> —George W. Bush (president, 2001–)

## ![] Foreign Affairs

"This foreign policy stuff is a little frustrating."

> —George W. Bush

"Well, he got this new globe for Christmas."

> —Bob Dole (1996 presidential nominee), on *Late Night with Conan O'Brien*, commenting on George W. Bush's knowledge of international relations

"I will have a foreign-handed foreign policy."

> —George W. Bush, during the 2000
> presidential campaign

## 🐘 Foreign Imports

"It is clear our nation is reliant upon big foreign oil. More and more of our imports come from over-seas."

> —George W. Bush

## 🐘 France

"France is like an aging actress of the 1940s. She's still dining out on her looks, but doesn't have the face for it."

> —John McCain (senator from Arizona, 1987–)

"The only way we'll get the French to help is if they find truffles in Iraq."

> —Orrin Hatch (senator from Utah, 1977–)

## 🐘 Free

"Where did this idea come from that everybody deserves free education? Free medical care? Free whatever? It comes from Moscow. From Russia. It comes straight out of the pit of hell."

> —Debbie Riddle (Texas state representative, 2003–)

## 🐘 Free Enterprise System

"I think that the free enterprise system is absolutely too important to be left to the voluntary action of the marketplace."

> —Richard Kelly (representative from Florida, 1975–1980)

## 🐘 Freedom Fries

"This is just to send a message to the troops to say that here in the Capitol, we are not happy."

> —Bob Ney (representative from Ohio, 1995–). Ney, chairman of the House Administration Committee, ordered the replacement of the word *French* with *freedom* on all House menu items

## 🐘 Fundraising

"I have a reputation for being strait-laced, but actually I come from a very tough state. In Utah—you think it's easy raising money from people who are all sober?"

> —Orrin Hatch (senator from Utah, 1977–)

## 🐘 Gag Orders

"If I'm the president, we're going to have emergency room care. We're going to have gag orders."

> —George W. Bush during the third
> presidential debate in 2000

## 🐘 Gay Marriage

"In every society, the definition of marriage has not, to my knowledge, included homosexuality. . . . It's not, you know, man on child, man on dog, or whatever the case may be."

> —Rick Santorum (senator from
> Pennsylvania, 1995–)

"I think that gay marriage should be between a man and a woman."

> —Arnold Schwarzenegger (governor of California, 2003–)

"Marriage is very simple: one man and one woman. Not two men or three men or four men or one man or one woman or two women and three women."

> —Bill Frist (senator from Tennessee, 1995–)

## 🐘 Georgia State Flag

"Pickup trucks, deer hunting, barefoot girls, and boiled peanuts—that's what that flag represents. Nobody looks at it as a symbol of hate."

> —Eric Johnson (Georgia state senator, 1995–), on the Georgia state flag, which features a large Confederate symbol

## 🐘 Getting Pillared

"I don't want to win? If that were the case, why the heck am I on the bus sixteen hours a day, shaking thousands of hands, giving thousands of speeches, getting pillared in the press and cartoons, and still staying on message to win?"

> —George W. Bush (president 2001–), during the 2000 presidential campaign

## 🐘 Gigantic

"We believe this is a gigantic first step."

> —George Gekas (representative from Pennsylvania, 1987–2002), meeting with seven-foot, two-inch Dikembe Mutombo of the Philadelphia Seventy-Sixers to discuss health care

## 🐘 Newt Gingrich

"It's clear that Mr. Gingrich is off his meds and out of therapy."

> —Richard Armitage (deputy secretary of state, 2001–), after Newt Gingrich criticized Secretary of State Colin Powell

"You know, he will go on and on whether he knows what he's talking about or not."

> —Marianne Gingrich (then-wife of Newt Gingrich), interrupting his pontifications about American history during a tour of the White House conducted by Hillary Rodham Clinton

## 🐘 Golf

"I know I am getting better at golf because I am hitting fewer spectators."

—Gerald Ford (president, 1974–1977)

"I always throw my golf club in the direction I'm going."

—Ronald Reagan (president, 1981–1989)

## 🐘 Good Man

"Laura and I are proud to call John and Michelle Engler our friends. I know you're proud to call him governor. What a good man the Englers are."

—George W. Bush

## 🐘 Al Gore

"Al Gore couldn't be more phony if he were a professional Al Gore impersonator."

—Dennis Miller (Republican political activist and humorist)

"You'd think a guy who could raise tobacco, slop hogs, build homes, invent the Internet, and inspire a best-selling novel and movie—all by the time he was twenty-eight—could afford to give more than $353 a year to charity."

> —Jim Nicholson (chairman, Republican
> National Committee, 1997–2001)

"Having been called charismatically challenged myself, I have a lot of sympathy."

> —Gerald Ford (president, 1974–1977)

## Government

"The government's view of the economy can be summed up in a few short phrases: If it moves, tax it. If it keeps moving, regulate it. And if it stops moving, subsidize it."

> —Ronald Reagan

"Giving money and power to government is like giving whiskey and car keys to teenage boys."

> —P. J. O'Rourke (author and commentator)

"I know something about being a government. And you've got a good one."

> —George W. Bush, campaigning for
> Arkansas Governor Mike Huckabee

"I don't want to abolish government. I simply want to reduce it to the size where I can drag it into the bathroom and drown it in the bathtub."

> —Grover Norquist (director, Americans for Tax Reform)

"The nine most terrifying words in the English language are 'I'm from the government and I'm here to help.'"

> —Ronald Reagan

## Grammatical Errors

"He doesn't make *that* many."

> —Laura Bush, asked on *Larry King Live* if she is bothered by her husband's grammatical errors

## Great Depression

"Many people have left their jobs for the more profitable one of selling apples."

> —Herbert Hoover (president, 1929–1933), on December 2, 1930

# 🐘 Group Sex

"I never lived my life to be a politician. I never lived my life to be the governor of California."

> —Arnold Schwarzenegger (governor of California, 2003–), on a 1977 *Oui* magazine article in which he bragged about participating in orgies

"Obviously, I've made statements that were ludicrous and crazy and outrageous and all those things because that's the way I always was. I was always that way, because otherwise I wouldn't have done the things that I did in my career, including the bodybuilding and the show business and all those things."

> —Arnold Schwarzenegger

# 🐘 Guests

"Last night was a very special evening at the White House. And I'm pleased to say that none of the silverware is missing."

> —Dick Cheney (vice president, 2001–), joking at a Republican Governor's Association dinner at the White House

"Ladies and gentlemen, Republican extremists, Democrats and other nonessentials, subpoenaed guests."

> —Colin Powell (former chairman, Joint Chiefs of Staff), in 1996, at the Alfala Club Dinner. The "subpoenaed guest" was Hillary Rodham Clinton.

## Guns

"An unloaded little tenny pistol."

> —Darrell Issa (representative from California, 2001–), discounting his conviction for possession of an unregistered gun. The *San Francisco Chronicle* reported that the gun was a loaded, .25-caliber semiautomatic pistol with 44 bullets.

"The sound of our guns is the sound of freedom."

> —Jeb Bush (governor of Florida, 1999–), at an NRA convention

## 🐘 Hanging

"I want to thank you for taking time out of your day to come and witness my hanging."

> —George W. Bush, joking at the unveiling of his portrait in the Texas state capitol

## 🐘 Health

"I haven't felt this good since I threw up on the Japanese prime minister."

> —George H. W. Bush (president, 1989–1993), while eating salsa

"Except for the occasional heart attack, I never felt better."

> —Dick Cheney, joking at the Radio and Television Correspondents' Association dinner

"The best activities for your health are pumping and humping."

> —Arnold Schwarzenegger (governor of California, 2003–)

"I can report that when they got in there they didn't find any pregnant chads at all."

> —Dick Cheney, joking about his heart surgery

## 🐘 Hillary

"If you are that gifted with money, will you promise to seek a seat on the Finance Committee?"

> —George F. Will (syndicated columnist and television commentator), on Hillary Rodham Clinton's transformation of a $1,000 investment in cattle futures into a $100,000 payoff

"When this Hillary gets to the Senate, she will be one of one hundred, and we won't let her forget it."

> —Trent Lott (senator from Mississippi, 1995–)

## 🐘 Hillary's Book

"I will not read it, I will not buy it, I will not subsidize Hillary Clinton's retirement. . . . Obviously this is a fictional version of what happened in the White House for eight years."

—Jim Bunning (senator from Kentucky, 1999–), on Hillary Rodham Clinton's book, *Living History*

## 🐘 Hispanically

"A lot of times in the rhetoric, people forget the facts. And the facts are that thousands of small businesses—Hispanically owned or otherwise—pay taxes at the highest marginal rate."

—George W. Bush (president, 2001–)

## 🐘 Hobbies

"A hobby I enjoy is mapping the human genome. I hope one day I can clone another Dick Cheney. Then I won't have to do anything."

—George W. Bush, joking at the Gridiron Dinner

## 🐘 Home

"It's time for Bill, Hillary, and Al to go home—if they can just figure out where home is."

> —Orrin Hatch (senator from Utah, 1977–),
> during the 2000 presidential campaign

## 🐘 Homocidal Maniacs

"We know who the homocidal maniacs are. They are the ones cheering and dancing right now. We should invade their countries, kill their leaders, and convert them to Christianity."

> —Ann Coulter (syndicated columnist and
> television commentator), on September
> 13, 2001. Coulter was fired from *National
> Review Online* for this column. She called
> the editors, Jonah Goldberg and Rich
> Lowry, "girly boys."

## 🐘 Homosexuals

"When it comes to sex, I don't give a shit what anyone's trip is."

> —Arnold Schwarzenegger

"Recently, I posed for a gay magazine, which caused some comment. But it doesn't bother me. Gay people are fighting the same kind of stereotyping that bodybuilders are. People have certain misconceptions about them just as they do about us. I have absolutely no hangups about the fag business; though it may bother some bodybuilders, it doesn't bother me."

> —Arnold Schwarzenegger, in a 1977 interview in *Oui* magazine

"I don't want this country to go that way. You know what happened to the Greeks. Homosexuality destroyed them. Sure, Aristotle was a homo; we all know that. So was Socrates."

> —Richard Nixon, expressing his view that the Meathead on *All in the Family* was bisexual

## Hostility

"We cannot let terrorists and rogue nations hold this nation hostile or hold our allies hostile."

> —George W. Bush

## ⭐ House Staining

"The administation I'll bring is a group of men and women who are focused on what's best for America, honest men and women, decent men and women, women who will see service to our country as a great privilege and who will not stain the house."

> —George W. Bush, in a 2000 Republican presidential debate

## ⭐ How Government Works

"I am mindful of the difference between the executive branch and the legislative branch. I assured all four of these leaders that I know the difference, and that difference is they pass the laws and I execute them."

> —George W. Bush, one month before his presidential inauguration

## ⭐ Human Fallacy

"I am a person who recognizes the fallacy of humans."

> —George W. Bush, on *Oprah* during the 2000 presidential campaign

# 🐘 Saddam Hussein

"The war on terror involves Saddam Hussein because of the nature of Saddam Hussein, the history of Saddam Hussein, and his willingness to terrorize himself."

>—George W. Bush

"After all, this is the guy who tried to kill my dad."

>—George W. Bush

"President Bush should drop an atomic bomb on Baghdad."

>—Patrick Landry (1999 congressional candidate from Louisiana). According to Landry, "If it saves lives, we should not take any military option off the table."

# 🐘 Hypocrisy

"I play fairly high stakes. I adhere to the law. I don't play the milk money. I don't put my family at risk, and I don't owe anyone anything."

>—Bill Bennett (author of *The Book of Virtues*), on reports that he lost $8 million in casino gambling. A few days later, Bennett announced, "My gambling days are over."

"I don't bet, and I don't gamble. I just enjoy watching horses running."

> —Pat Robertson (founder of the Christian Coalition and 1988 presidential candidate)

## 🐘 Hypothetical Questions

"If James Carville and Geraldo Rivera were both drowning, and you could only save one, would you read the paper or eat lunch?"

> —Mitch Daniels (director, Office of Management and Budget, 2001–2003), imagining a conversation with his college-age daughter

"If I were to lose my mind right now and pick up one of you and dash your head against the floor and kill you, would that be right?"

> —Alan Keyes (2000 presidential candidate)

# Images

"We're trying to get good pictures. Don't worry very much about what I say."

—Bob Dole (1996 presidential nominee)

# Importance

"The most important job is not to be governor, or first lady in my case."

—George W. Bush

# Inauguration

"Sir, you have the right to remain silent."

—Pat Buchanan (1996 presidential candidate), saying that his first act as president—as the nation's chief law enforcement officer—would be to arrest Bill Clinton

# Incognito

"He never promised me a Rose Garden."

—John McCain (senator from Arizona, 1987–), on the fact that President Bush signed the McCain-Feingold campaign finance legislation without any fanfare

"I only have on one layer of makeup. I'm incognito."

> —Katherine Harris (Florida secretary of state, 1999–2002), upon being recognized while shopping at Target

## 🐘 Inconsistency

"The senator has got to understand if he's going to have—he can't have it both ways. He can't take the high horse and then claim the low road."

> —George W. Bush (president, 2001–), on Senator John McCain, during the 2000 presidential campaign

## 🐘 Inebriation

"It was just inebriating what Midland was all about then."

> —George W. Bush, reminiscing about his childhood in Midland, Texas

## 🐘 Informed Voting

"Does anybody know where H-236 is? I'd like to know where it is before I vote for it."

> —Don Young (representative from Alaska, 1973–), before voting to name a room in the Capitol for former House Majority Leader Dick Armey

## 🐘 Inhaling

"I have inhaled, exhaled everything."

> —Arnold Schwarzenegger (governor of California, 2003–), on his drug use

## 🐘 Intelligence

"These stories about my intellectual capacity really get under my skin. You know, for a while I even thought my staff believed it. There on my schedule first thing every morning it said, 'Intelligence Briefing.'"

> —George W. Bush, joking at the Radio-TV Correspondents' Dinner

"I don't see why the legislature should be in the business of artifical intelligence, real intelligence, or any intelligence at all."

> —Hunt Downer (Louisiana state representative, 1975–2003), in response to proposed spending for computer software

## 🐘 Intercontinentalism

"The guy memorizes four words, and he plays like he's intercontinental."

> —George W. Bush, after NBC reporter David Gregory asked a question in French to the president of France

## 🐘 Internal Revenue Service

"I want to make sure he is a ruthless son of a bitch, do what he's told, that every income tax I want to see I see, that he will go after our enemies and not our friends. Now it's as simple as that. If he doesn't, he doesn't get the job."

> —Richard Nixon (president, 1969–1974), on appointing an IRS Commissioner

"What does that candyass think I sent him over there for?"

> —Richard Nixon, on the refusal of George Schultz, his Secretary of the Treasury, to authorize tax audits of Nixon's enemies

"Only in Washington would anyone call the IRS a 'service.'"

> —Steve Forbes (2000 presidential candidate)

## 🐘 Internet

"Thank you for your e-mail. This Internet of yours is a wonderful invention."

> —George W. Bush, to Al Gore during the 2000 presidential campaign

## 🐘 Internment

"We were at war. They were an endangered species."

> —Howard Coble (representative from North Carolina, 1985–), stating his conviction that interning Japanese Americans during World War II was for their own safety

# 🐘 Iowa

"Of all states that understands local control of schools, Iowa is such a state."

—George W. Bush, in Council Bluffs, Iowa

# 🐘 Iraq

"I don't do quagmires."

—Donald Rumsfeld (secretary of defense, 2001–), searching for a word to describe the situation in Iraq

"We ended the rule of one of history's worst tyrants, and in so doing, we not only freed the American people, we made our own people more secure."

—George W. Bush

"You're free. And freedom is beautiful. And, you know, it'll take time to restore chaos and order—order out of chaos. But we will."

—George W. Bush

"My answer is: Bring them on."

—George W. Bush, on the prospect of Iraqi militants attacking American forces

## 🐘 Japan

"For a century and a half now, America and Japan have formed one of the great and enduring alliances of modern times."

> —George W. Bush (a history major at Yale)

## 🐘 Jerusalem

"[I support] a united and indivisible Jerusalem as the capital of Utah."

> —Orrin Hatch (senator from Utah, 1977–), during the 2000 presidential campaign

## 🐘 Jews

"*Newsweek* is totally—it's all run by Jews and dominated by them in their editorial pages. The *New York Times*, the *Washington Post*, totally Jewish, too."

> —Richard Nixon (president, 1969–1974), in a 1972 conversation with Billy Graham

"I always see two Jewish communities in America. One of deep intellect and one of shallow, superficial intellect."

> —Dick Armey (representative from Texas, 1985–2002)

"You know, it's a funny thing. Every one of the bastards that are out for legalizing marijuana is Jewish. What the Christ is the matter with the Jews, Bob? What is the matter with them? I suppose it is because most of them are psychiatrists."

> —Richard Nixon to Bob Haldeman, his White House chief of staff

##  Kennedy Family Gatherings

"Well, first of all, we always have major arguments up there in Hyannisport when we got together for those dinners—or in Washington—because the Kennedys never want to sit to the far right. So we have a problem right there with the seating arrangement."

> —Arnold Schwarzenegger, on his relationship with the Kennedy family

"I think you should train with weights three times a day. He don't believe in that. So we fight over those things. So those are the kinds of things we argue."

> —Arnold Schwarzenegger (governor of California, 2003–), on his wife's uncle, Ted Kennedy

## 🐘 John Kerry

"One is reminded that [John Kerry] is really just a better-looking Ted Kennedy, a richer Michael Dukakis."

> —Laura Ingraham (radio talk show host)

"If his wife doesn't trust him, why should you?"

> —Sean Hannity (radio and television talk show host), on the fact that Senator John Kerry's extremely wealthy wife, Teresa Heinz Kerry, requested that he sign a prenuptial agreement

**Kids**

"Some of these kids in it would be better off sitting on a piano bench at a whorehouse than where they are now."

> —Haley Barbour (governor of Mississippi, 2004–), at Sacred Heart Elementary School in DeSoto County, Mississippi, on the poor home situation faced by many Head Start children

## Knowledge

"Look, I don't care about the numbers. I know the facts."

> —George W. Bush, responding to economists debating the economic impact of September 11

## Kyoto Treaty

"Kyoto means 'pink slip' in French."

> —Richard Pombo (representative from California, 1993–), on an international treaty to restrict global warming

## 🐘 Kenneth Lay

"I'd say you were a carnival barker, except that wouldn't be fair to carnival barkers."

> —Peter Fitzgerald (senator from Illinois, 1999–), to Enron chief executive officer Kenneth Lay

## 🐘 Learning

"Reading is the basics for all learning."

> —George W. Bush, trumpeting his "Reading First" initiative

## 🐘 Legislation

"We accomplished a lot today. We commended a winery. Let's go home."

> —John Hainkel (Louisiana state senate, 1988–)

"This $75,000 to send rodeo contestants to attend the National Rodeo: does that include popcorn?"

> —Tony Perkins (Louisiana state representative, 1996–2003), on a state appropriations bill

## Legs

"I wish reporters would ask me more about what's in my head and less about what's between my legs."

> —Karen Kerin (a 2000 transgender congressional candidate from Vermont)

## Liberals

"Liberals aren't stupid. It's just that most of what they know is not true."

> —Ronald Reagan (president, 1981–1989)

"You can play golf with liberals. I just don't want them in power."

> —Sean Hannity (television and radio talk show host)

"Liberals hate America, they hate 'flag-wavers,' they

hate abortion opponents, they hate all religions except Islam (post 9/11). Even Islamic terrorists don't hate America like liberals do. They don't have the energy. If they had that much energy, they'd have indoor plumbing by now."

> —Ann Coulter (syndicated columnist and television commentator)

"Liberals thrive on the attractions of snobbery. Only when you appreciate the powerful driving force of snobbery in the liberals' worldview do all their preposterous counterintuitive arguments make sense. They promote immoral destructive behavior because they are snobs, they embrace criminals because they are snobs, they oppose tax cuts because they are snobs, they adore the environment because they are snobs."

> —Ann Coulter

"Liberals hate religion because politics is a religion substitute for liberals and they can't stand the competition."

> —Ann Coulter

"A liberal is someone who owes a great deal to his fellow man, which debt he proposes to pay off with your money."

> —G. Gordon Liddy (radio talk show host)

"Please understand that I'm not saying that liberals like Bill Clinton and Al Gore and Tom Daschle and Dick Gephardt and many of the elitists in academic and the media are evil. I'm saying they have a disturbing habit of winking at evil—of ignoring it, or turning a blind eye to it."

> —Sean Hannity (radio and television talk show host)

## 🐘 Life

"It's important for us to explain to our nation that life is important. It's not only life of babies, but it's life of children living in, you know, the dark dungeons of the Internet."

> —George W. Bush (president, 2001–)

## 🐘 Lipstick

"If there was ever a situation in which they attempted to put lipstick on a pig, this is it."

> —Duf Sundheim (chairman, California Republican Party), on Democratic Party support for Cruz Bustamante during the 2003 California recall election

## 🐘 Listening

"I promise you I will listen to what has been said here, even though I wasn't here."

> —George W. Bush, on his way out the door at the President's Economic Forum in Waco, Texas

## 🐘 Looks

"There you are. You look just like yourself."

> —George W. Bush, upon seeing ESPN analyst Kirk Herbstreit at the White House

# 🐘 Loopholes

"You personally, with your personal income tax, have the biggest loophole. I can drive my Hummer through it."

> —Arnold Schwarzenegger, to fellow gubernatorial candidate Arianna Huffington, in a debate during the 2003 California recall election

# 🐘 Louisiana

"Every four years Baton Rouge cries out to Louisiana and says, 'Send us your best.' And we are it. That is scary as you look around and see some of us."

> —Vic Stelly (Louisiana state representative, 1987–)

"It's important for Louisianians to elect someone who reflects their values—someone who's not for the morning-after pill, who's not for a needle-exchange program, someone who's not for discontinuing funding for the Boy Scouts."

> —Bill Kearney (campaign adviser to Suzanne Terrell, senatorial candidate from Louisiana, 2002)

## 🐘 Love

"The U.S. Senate is a special place. I love all of you, and especially your wives."

> —Strom Thurmond (senator from South Carolina, 1954–2002), in his farewell speech on September 24, 2002. Thurmond was ninety-nine at the time.

## 🐘 Marin County Hot-Tubbers

"Call off the dogs, please . . . I am chastised and will never use *hot tub* and *Marin County* in the same sentence again."

> —George H. W. Bush (president, 1989–1993), apologizing for calling "American Taliban" John Walker Lindh "some misguided Marin County hot-tubber"

## 🐘 Marketing

"From a marketing point of view, you don't introduce new products in August."

> —Andrew Card Jr. (chief of staff to President George W. Bush, 2001–), explaining why the Bush administration delayed launching its campaign to convince the American public to support mobilization against Iraq

## 🐘 Me

"Actually, I—this may sound a little West Texas to you, but I like it. When I'm talking about—when I'm talking about myself, and when he's talking about myself, all of us are talking about me."

> —George W. Bush

"To be blunt—and God watch over Paul's soul—I am a 99 percent improvement over Paul Wellstone."

> —Norm Coleman (senator from Minnesota, 2003–), referring to his predecessor, who was killed in a plane crash in October 2002. Coleman quickly apologized.

## 🐘 Media

"They admit they're anti-business, pro–big government, anti-family, and anti-religion."

> —Reed Irvine (chairman emeritus, Accuracy in Media)

"Who's gonna give me a TV show? I didn't work for an impeached, disbarred president who was held in contempt by a federal judge. That's what they look for in objective reporters."

> —Ann Coulter (syndicated columnist and television commentator)

"I understand that the press sometimes has to put politicians under a microscope. But when they use a proctoscope, that's going too far."

> —Richard Nixon (president, 1969–1974)

## 🐘 Medical Diagnosis

"Right here, Mr. President, is where your tax cut is stuck. The Republicans can't quite swallow it, and the Democrats can't cough it up."

> —Bill Frist (senator from Tennessee, 1995–), a medical doctor, pointing to the esophagus on a medical chart

## 🐘 Medical Malpractice

"The trial lawyers are very politically powerful. . . .
But here in Texas we took them on and got some
good medical—medical malpractice."

> —George W. Bush

## 🐘 Mediocrity

"To those of you who received honors, awards, and
distinctions, I say, well done. And to the C students, I say: You, too, can be president."

> —George W. Bush, accepting an honorary
> doctorate from Yale University, his alma
> mater

## 🐘 Middle East

"I understand that the unrest in the Middle East
creates unrest through throughout the region."

> —George W. Bush

## 🐘 Military Base Closings

"Sure, I'm going to protect Portsmouth. Why don't we turn it into an ethanol plant and ship the corn out from Iowa?"

> —John McCain (senator from Arizona, 1987–), sarcastically answering a question whether he would maintain the military base in Portsmouth, New Hampshire

## 🐘 Military Tribunals

"Someone is watching too much *L.A. Law*."

> —Donald Rumsfeld (secretary of defense, 2001–), responding to questions about military detainees in Guatanomo Bay. Rumsfeld was apparently unaware that *L.A. Law* has been off the air since May 1994.

## 🐘 Milk

"Milk is for babies. When you grow up, you have to drink beer."

> —Arnold Schwarzenegger (governor of California, 2003–)

## 🐘 Missiles

"I'm not going to fire a $2 million missile at a ten dollar empty tent and hit a camel in the butt."

—George W. Bush (president, 2001–)

## 🐘 Misunderestimation

"They misunderestimated me."

—George W. Bush

## 🐘 Moderates

"I'm getting a little tired of politicians trying to prove how 'moderate' and centrist they are by taking more of my money and freedom. Where's the center—somewhere between Lenin and Stalin?"

—Ann Coulter (syndicated columnist and television commentator)

## 🐘 Monica

"I would be looking up from a pool of blood and hearing [my wife] ask, 'How do I reload this thing?'"

—Dick Armey (representative from Texas, 1982–2002), asked what he would do if he were in Bill Clinton's situation during the Monica Lewinsky scandal

## 🐘 More Few

"Will the highways on the Internet become more few?"

—George W. Bush

## 🐘 Motherhood

"I may be the only mother in America who knows exactly what their child is up to all the time."

—Barbara Bush

"She treats him like he's fifteen years old."

—George H. W. Bush (president, 1989–1993), on his wife's scolding of the forty-third president of the United States

## 🐘 Motivation

"When you have 'em by the balls, their hearts and minds will follow."

—Charles Colson (Nixon White House staffer)

## 🐘 My Speech

"And so, in my State of the—my State of the Union—or state—my speech to the nation, whatever you want to call it, speech to the nation—I asked Americans to give four thousand years—four thousand hours over the next—the rest of our life—of service to America. That's what I asked—four thousand hours."

—George W. Bush

## 🐘 Naps

"Is the country still here?"

—Calvin Coolidge (president, 1923–1929), waking up from a long nap

## 🐘 Narcissism

"Somewhere in this group is the next Karl Rove."

—Karl Rove (George W. Bush's chief political adviser), at a college Republicans' conference

# 🐘 National Football League

"I don't think he's been that good from the get-go. I think what we've had here is a little social concern in the NFL. The media has been very desirous that a black quarterback do well. There is a little hope invested in McNabb, and he got a lot of credit for the performance of this team that he didn't deserve. The defense carried the team."

> —Rush Limbaugh (radio talk show host), on Donovan McNabb, quarterback of the Philadelphia Eagles. On his radio show, Rush said, "All this has become the tempest that it is because I must have been right about something. If I wasn't right, there wouldn't be this cacophony of outrage that has sprung up in the sportswriting community." Three days after making the statement, Limbaugh resigned from his position at ESPN.

# 🐘 NATO

"Why not? I haven't thought about the nuance of it."

> —George W. Bush (president, 2001–), asked at a summit with Russian President Vladimir Putin if he favored admitting Russia to NATO

## 🐘 Natural Gas

"Natural gas is hemispheric. I like to call it hemispheric in nature because it is a product that we can find in our neighborhoods."

> —George W. Bush

## 🐘 Nature

"You can't just let nature run wild."

> —Walter Hickel (governor of Alaska, 1967–1969, 1991–1994), defending his support for a plan by Alaska state government to kill hundreds of wolves

## 🐘 Negativity

"It's negative to think about blowing each other up. That's not a positive thought."

> —George W. Bush, at a summit meeting with Russian President Vladmir Putin

## 🐘 Negroes

"The Negro cannot count forever on the kind of restraint that's thus far left him free to clog the streets, disrupt traffic, and interfere with other men's rights."

> —Jesse Helms (senator from North Carolina, 1973–2002), in 1963

## 🐘 Richard Nixon

"As much ribbing as I've taken, I guess I ought to use it for something."

> —Richard M. Nixon (candidate for Alabama Commissioner of Agriculture in 2002), on his name

"I wouldn't trust Nixon from here to that phone."

> —Barry Goldwater (1964 presidential nominee)

"Nixon was always being attacked sexually. It was always said that he was a fag and that he had no sexual relations with his wife for fifteen years and that was why he liked power. And Hitler had only one ball, and that was why he wanted to conquer the world."

> —Arnold Schwarzenegger (governor of California, 2003–), in a 1977 interview in *Oui* magazine

## 🐘 North Vietnam

"We should declare war on North Vietnam. We should pave the whole country and put parking stripes on it and still be home for Christmas."

> —Barry Goldwater (1964 presidential nominee)

## 🐘 Nuclear Energy

"If you set aside Three Mile Island and Chernobyl, the safety record of nuclear energy is really very good."

> —Paul O'Neill (secretary of the treasury, 2001–2003)

## Oil

"Why not go to war just for oil? We need oil. What do Hollywood celebrities imagine fuels their private jets? How do they think their cocaine is delivered to them?"

> —Ann Coulter (syndicated columnist and television commentator), at the 2003 Conservative Political Action Committee convention

## Old Sayings

"There's an old saying in Tennessee—I know it's in Texas, probably in Tennessee—that says, fool me once, shame on—shame on you. Fool me—you can't get fooled again."

> —George W. Bush

## Tip O'Neill

"Fat, bloated, and out of control—just like the federal budget."

> —John LeBoutillier (representative from New York, 1981–1982), on then–House Speaker Tip O'Neill. Asked his response, O'Neill said, "I wouldn't know him from a cord of wood."

## 🐘 Opponents

"People can be weird and not be traitors."

> —Newt Gingrich (representative from
> Georgia, 1981–1999)

## 🐘 Opportunistic Society

"The public education system in America is one of
the most important foundations of our democracy.
After all, it is where children learn to be respon-
sible citizens, and learn to have the skills neces-
sary to take advantage of our fantastic
opportunistic society."

> —George W. Bush (president, 2001–)

## 🐘 Orders

"When the guy from the White House tells you to
take your tie off, you don't ask why."

> —Brian Bosma (Indiana state
> representative, 1987–), who was asked by
> a staff member for President George W.
> Bush to remove his tie to make the
> audience look more ordinary

## 🐘 Osama bin Laden

"[Osama bin Laden] is either alive and well or alive and not well or not alive."

> —Donald Rumsfeld (secretary of defense, 2001–)

## 🐘 Pacemakers

"We'll let our friends be the peacekeepers and the great country called America will be the pacemakers."

> —George W. Bush

## 🐘 Parents

"They're horrified, actually."

> —Ari Fleischer (White House press secretary, 2001–2003), asked if his parents are proud of his job

## 🐘 The Past

"I think we agree, the past is over."

>—George W. Bush, on his meeting with
>Senator John McCain after McCain
>dropped out of the 2000 presidential race

## 🐘 Peaceful Coexistence

"I know the human being and fish can coexist
peacefully."

>—George W. Bush

## 🐘 Pension Protection

"If this legislation was in place a year ago, Enron's
hardworking employees would not have had to
shed their skivvies in *Playboy* to supplement their
retirements."

>—Mark Foley (representative from Florida,
>1995–)

## 🐘 Personal Attacks

"You need a little more decaf."

>—Arnold Schwarzenegger to fellow
>California gubernatorial candidate
>Arianna Huffington, during a debate

"I just realized that I have the perfect part for you in *Terminator 4*."

> —Arnold Schwarzenegger to Arianna Huffington, during a debate. In *Terminator 3*, Schwarzenegger's character flushed a woman character down the toilet.

## 🐘 Pies

"We need to make the pie higher."

> —George W. Bush, during the 2000 presidential campaign

## 🐘 Plans

"Get a good night's sleep and don't bug anybody without asking me."

> —Richard Nixon (president, 1969–1974) to Clark MacGregor, manager of his 1972 reelection campaign

## 🐘 Politicians

"Ninety percent of the politicians give the other 10 percent a bad name."

> —Henry Kissinger (secretary of state, 1971–1976)

"The worst thing a politician can be is dull. At least I'm interesting."

—Richard Nixon

##  Politics

"Politics would be a helluva good business if it weren't for the goddamned people."

—Richard Nixon

"Politics is mostly pill-taking."

—Thomas B. Reed (representative from Maine, 1877–1900)

"Politics is supposed to be the second oldest profession. I have come to realize that it bears a very close resemblance to the first."

—Ronald Reagan (president, 1981–1989)

"Politics is not a bad profession. If you succeed, there are many rewards. If you disgrace yourself, you can always write a book."

—Ronald Reagan

## 🐘 Poor Killers

"First, let me make it very clear, poor people aren't necessarily killers. Just because you happen to be not rich doesn't mean you're willing to kill."

> —George W. Bush (president, 2001–)

## 🐘 Popular Culture

"I don't even know those two kids. Don't wanna know 'em."

> —George H. W. Bush (president, 1989–1993), asked whether Justin Timberlake and Britney Spears should resume their romance

## 🐘 Posse

"Contrary to my image as a Texan with two guns on my side, I'm more comfortable with a posse."

> —George W. Bush, speaking to Czech President Vaclav Havel in Prague for a NATO meeting

## 🐘 Posturing

"As far as the legal hassling and wrangling and posturing in Florida, I would suggest you talk to our team in Florida led by Jim Baker."

—George W. Bush

## 🐘 Poverty

"Half the world does not know the joy of wearing cotton underwear."

—Phil Gramm (senator from Texas, 1985–2002)

## 🐘 Power

"The California crunch really is the result of not enough power-generating plants and then not enough power to power the power of generating plants."

—George W. Bush

"I was always dreaming about very powerful people —dictators and things like that. I was always just impressed by people who could be remembered for hundreds of years, or even, like Jesus, be for thousands of years remembered."

> —Arnold Schwarzenegger (governor of
> California, 2003–), in the 1977
> documentary, *Pumping Iron*

"Power corrupts. Absolute power is kind of neat."

> —John Lehman (secretary of the Navy,
> 1981–1987)

"Power is the great aphrodisiac."

> —Henry Kissinger, (secretary of state,
> 1971–1976)

## Predecessors

"I am mindful not only of preserving executive powers for myself, but for predecessors as well."

> —George W. Bush, nine days after taking
> office

## Presidency

"I don't want to be the president. I want my Blackberry."

> —Jeb Bush (governor of Florida, 1999–)

"Any man who wants to be president is either an ego-maniac or crazy."

> —Dwight David Eisenhower (president, 1953–1961)

"Listen, I'm just as shocked as you are that I'm sitting here talking about the presidency."

> —George W. Bush, on *The News Hour with Jim Lehrer* during the 2000 presidential campaign

## Principles

"If you don't stand for anything, you don't stand for anything!"

> —George W. Bush

"If you're sick and tired of the politics of cynicism and polls and principles, come and join this campaign."

> —George W. Bush, during the 2000 presidential campaign

## Priorities

"Our priorities is our faith."

> —George W. Bush

## 🐘 Problems

"We'd like to avoid problems, because when he have problems, we can have troubles."

> —Wesley Bolin (governor of Arizona, 1977–1978)

## 🐘 Processing

"Oftentimes, we live in a processed world—you know, people focus on the process and not results."

> —George W. Bush

## 🐘 Progress

"We don't want to go back to tomorrow; we want to go forward."

> —Dan Quayle (vice president, 1989–1993)

"We're not backpedaling. We're front-pedaling."

> —Mike Foster (governor of Louisiana, 1995–2003), after floating a trial balloon on the state budget

## ♦ Propaganda

"The office is done. It's over. What do you want, blood?"

> —Donald Rumsfeld (secretary of defense, 2001–), on abolishing a controversial propaganda division

## Proposition 13

"I told Warren that if he mentions Proposition 13 one more time, he has to do five hundred sit-ups."

> —Arnold Schwarzenegger, referring to the statement made by Warren Buffet, his chief economic adviser, that California's Proposition 13 (which limits property taxes) should be repealed

## ♦ Public Opinion

"The average American doesn't know the difference between a Contra and a caterpillar or between a Sandinista and a sardine."

> —John East (senator from North Carolina, 1981–1986), supporting U.S. military aid to the pro-American contras in Nicaragua

## 🐘 Qualifications

"I'm not smart enough to lie."

> —Ronald Reagan (president, 1981–1989),
> asked what qualified him to be president

"I do remain confident in Linda. She'll make a fine labor secretary. From what I've read in the press accounts, she's perfectly qualified."

> —George W. Bush (president, 2001–) on
> January 8, 2001, announcing the
> nomination of Linda Chavez as Secretary
> of Labor. Chavez later asked that her
> nomination be withdrawn because of her
> illegal immigrant housekeepers.

"I am a thirty-two-year-old virgin—and proud of it."

> —Patrick Landry (1999 congressional
> candidate from Louisiana) during a
> candidate debate. Landry ran radio ads
> proclaiming, "I am a thirty-two-year-old
> virgin—because when I make a moral
> stand, I keep it."

"The fact that he is black and a minority has nothing to do with this sense that he is the best qualified at this time. I kept my word to the American people and to the Senate by picking the best man for the job on the merits."

> —George H. W. Bush (president, 1989–1993), nominating Clarence Thomas to the U.S. Supreme Court. Thomas had been a federal judge for sixteen months; he received a midlevel grade of "qualified" from the American Bar Association.

## ☭ Quickie

"My press release will read, 'Ros-Lehtinen does quickie with Secretary Powell.' I'm ready!"

> —Ileana Ros-Lehtinen (representative from Florida, 1989–), after being told that time was short during a congressional hearing with Secretary of State Colin Powell

## 🐘 Race Relations

"I don't understand how they can call me anti-Latino when I've made four movies in Mexico."

> —Arnold Schwarzenegger (governor of California, 2003–)

## 🐘 Racial Profiling

"I mean, there needs to be a wholesale effort against racial profiling, which is illiterate children."

> —George W. Bush, during his second debate with Al Gore

## 🐘 Reading

"You teach a child to read, and he or her will be able to pass a literacy test."

> —George W. Bush

"[Arkansas and Alabama] don't need fancy theories, or what may sound good. Science is not an art—I mean, reading is not an art. It's a science. We know what works."

> —George W. Bush

## 🐘 Reality

"I'm gonna talk about the ideal world, Chris. I've read—I understand reality. If you're asking me as the president, would I understand reality, I do."

> —George W. Bush, during the 2000 presidential campaign, to Chris Matthews of *Hardball*

## 🐘 Recall

"This is really embarrassing. I just forget our state governor's name, but I know that you will help me recall it."

> —Arnold Schwarzenegger

## 🐘 Regrets

"Probably wearing a red tie too many times."

> —George W. Bush, asked about his biggest mistake during his first one hundred days in office

## 🐘 Religious Killers

"I know you have had calls saying vote against this. Many have told me that if I vote for it, those religious people will kill me."

> —Danny Martiny (Louisiana state representative, 1994–2003), speaking on the floor of the Louisiana House about legislation decriminalizing certain sex acts done in private by consenting adults

## 🐘 Remembering

"The thing that's important for me to remember is what's the most important thing."

> —George W. Bush

## 🐘 Repugnancy

"To suggest I would stoop to an 'inappropriate relationship' to achieve legislative results is repugnant and sexist."

> —Deborah Steelman (a lobbyist and former official in the first Bush administration), who conceded having a sexual relationship with Congressman Bill

Thomas, chairman of the House Ways and Means Committee. Steelman routinely had business with Thomas's committee and steered financial contributions to his campaign.

## Retirement

"Now, we talked to Joan Hanover. She and her husband, George, were visiting with us. They are near retirement—retiring—in the process of retiring, meaning they're very smart, active, capable people who are retirement age and are retiring."

> —George W. Bush (president, 2001–)

## Roadblocks

"Security is the essential roadblock to achieving the road map to peace."

> —George W. Bush

## Roasts

"How can they roast toast?"

> —Trent Lott (senator from Mississippi, 1987–), joking at a dinner roast about losing his job as Senate majority leader

## 🐘 Romans

"Do you know what happened to the Romans? The last six Roman emperors were fags. . . . You know what happened to the popes? It's all right that popes were laying the nuns."

> —Richard Nixon (president, 1969–1974)

## 🐘 Donald Rumsfeld

"He thought I was some kind of airhead academic, and I thought he was rather an arrogant young member of Congress. Probably we were both right."

> —Dick Cheney (vice president 2001–), recalling his first encounter with Donald Rumsfeld, in 1968

## 🐘 Safety First

"You may be glad to know that the president is practicing safe snacks."

> —Laura Bush (first lady, 2001–), to Jay Leno, after her husband's run-in with a pretzel

## 🐘 Sanitation Workers

"I bet you can find statistics that say being a sanitation worker . . . is more dangerous than being a policeman or fireman. It's a dangerous job."

> —Mike Bloomberg (mayor of New York City, 2002–), during the 2001 campaign

## 🐘 Savages

"Whether they are rooting for the atheistic regimes of Stalin and Mao, satanic suicide bombers and terrorists, or the Central Park rapists, liberals always take the side of savages against civilization."

> —Ann Coulter (syndicated columnist and television commentator)

## 🐘 Secretaries

"I think any man in business would be foolish to fool around with his secretary. If it's somebody else's secretary, fine."

> —Barry Goldwater (1964 presidential nominee)

## 🐘 Segregation

"I want to say this about my state: When Strom Thurmond ran for president, we voted for him. We're proud of it. And if the rest of the country had followed our lead, we wouldn't have had all these problems over all these years, either."

> —Trent Lott (senator from Mississippi, 1987–), at Strom Thurmond's one hundredth birthday party. Thurmond ran for president in 1948 as a segregationist. The furor over Lott's remark forced him to resign as senate majority leader.

## 🐘 Self-Interest

"In other words, I don't think people ought to be compelled to make the decision which they think is best for their family."

> —George W. Bush, explaining why he opposes mandatory smallpox vaccinations

## 🐘 Self-Knowledge

"I think if you know what you believe, it makes it a lot easier to answer questions. I can't answer your question."

> —George W. Bush, asked whether he wished he could disavow any of his statements in the first 2000 presidential debate

## 🐘 Senators

"When they call the roll in the Senate, the Senators do not know whether to answer 'present' or 'not guilty.'"

> —Teddy Roosevelt (president, 1901–1909)

# 🐘 September 11

"I really believe that the pagans and the abortionists and the feminists and the gays and the lesbians who are actively trying to make that an alternative lifestyle, the ACLU, People for the American Way—all of them who have tried to secularize America—I point the finger in their face and say, 'You helped this happen.'"

> —Jerry Falwell (founder, Moral Majority), on *The 700 Club* with Pat Robertson on September 13, 2001

# 🐘 Sex and Politics

"Sex and politics are a lot alike. You don't have to be good at them to enjoy them."

> —Barry Goldwater (1964 presidential nominee)

# 🐘 Shovels

"Some of us are like a shovel brigade that follow a parade down Main Street cleaning up."

> —Donald Regan (chief of staff to President Reagan), on the Iceland summit meeting between Ronald Reagan and Mikhail Gorbachev in November 1986

## 🐘 Similarities

"We both use Colgate toothpaste."

> —George W. Bush (president, 2001–), asked
> at Camp David, Maryland, in February
> 2001 what he had in common with British
> Prime Minister Tony Blair

## 🐘 Singing

"I think I should get points for not doing Perry
Como."

> —Joe Scarborough (representative from
> Florida, 1995–2002), who played guitar
> with his band, Regular Joe, and often
> sang the alt-rock tune, "Teenage Dirtbag"
> ("Oh, how she rocks in Keds and tube
> socks / But she doesn't know who I am /
> And she doesn't give a damn about me /
> 'Cause I'm just a teenage dirtbag, baby").

## 🐘 Slaves

"It's very interesting when you think about it, the
slaves who left here to go to America, because of
their steadfast and their religion and their belief in
freedom, helped changed America."

> —George W. Bush, in Dakar, Senegal

## 🐘 Small Business Growth

"I understand small business growth. I was one."

—George W. Bush

## 🐘 Smooching

"We're in touch with our sexuality. What can I say?"

—John Sweeney (representative from New York, 1999–), commenting on a picture of him smooching with George W. Bush

## 🐘 Social Security

"There's not going to be enough people in the system to take advantage of people like me."

—George W. Bush

## 🐘 Solidarity

"If you're shoulder to shoulder with them, your hand is in their pocket."

—John Hainkel (Louisiana state senator, 1988–), to a lobbyist who proclaimed that he stood "shoulder to shoulder" with the administration on a bill

## 🐘 Sounding Off

"This is the kind of job when you come home at the end of the day, you really like to have someone to sound off to, and the plants just weren't doing it for me."

> —Christine Todd Whitman (EPA administrator, 2001–2003), announcing her resignation

## 🐘 Soundness

"I was alarmed at my doctor's report. He said I was sound as a dollar."

> —Ronald Reagan, during the 1980 presidential campaign

## 🐘 Sources

"Nobody believes the official spokesman—but everybody trusts an unidentified source."

> —Ron Ziegler (press secretary to President Nixon)

## 🐘 South African Sanctions

"Are the women of America prepared to give up all their jewelry?"

> —Donald Regan (chief of staff to President Reagan), asked to defend the Reagan administration's opposition to economic sanctions against South Africa

## 🐘 Southerners

"I wanna tell you, ladies and gentlemen, that there's not enough troops in the Army to force the Southern people to break down segregation and admit the nigger race into our theaters, into our swimming pools, into our homes, and into our churches."

> —Strom Thurmond (senator from South Carolina, 1953–2002), during the 1948 presidential campaign

## 🐘 Arlen Specter

"Arlen Specter is a jerk, but he's our jerk."

> —Paul Weyrich (Republican political activist), on the senior senator from Pennsylvania

## 🐘 Spouses

"She used to make me hamburgers. I've been eating salads for four months. I think I need Meals on Wheels."

> —Bob Dole (1996 Republican presidential nominee), on losing twenty-three pounds since his wife, Elizabeth, joined the U.S. Senate

## 🐘 State of the Union

"Our nation is at war, our economy is in recession, and the civilized world faces unprecedented dangers. Yet the state of the union has never been stronger."

> —George W. Bush, in his 2002 State of the Union Address

## 🐘 Statements

"[Mr. Nixon's latest statement] is the operative White House position—and all previous statements are inoperative."

> —Ron Ziegler (press secretary to President Nixon), during the Watergate affair

## States

"Every state's got them a couple of senators."

> —George W. Bush, encouraging members of
> the public to lobby their senators to
> support his medical liability reform plan

## Status Quo

"Only one thing would be worse than the status
quo. And that would be for the status quo to
become the norm."

> —Elizabeth Dole (2000 presidential
> candidate)

## Stewardship

"You're good stewards of the quality of the air."

> —George W. Bush (president, 2001–), in
> September 2003 at the Detroit Edison
> power plant in Monroe, Michigan. In
> 2001, the plant sent 102,700 tons of
> sulfur dioxide, 45,900 tons of nitrogen
> oxide, 810 pounds of mercury, and 17.6
> million tons of carbon dioxide into the air.

**Stress**

"There's a lot of stress involved after your house is underwater."

> —Scott McCallum (governor of Wisconsin, 2001–2003), traipsing through the flooded streets of Prairie du Chien, Wisconsin

 **Stupidity**

"As much as when you see a blond with great tits and a great ass, you say to yourself, 'Hey, she must be stupid or have nothing else to offer,' which maybe is the case many times. But then again there is the one that is as smart as her breasts look, great as her face looks, beautiful as her whole body looks gorgeous, you know, so people are shocked."

> —Arnold Schwarzenegger (governor of California, 2003–)

 **Subliminality**

"The idea of putting subliminable messages into ads is ridiculous."

> —George W. Bush, during the 2000 presidential campaign

"I don't think we need to be subliminable about the differences between our views on prescription drugs."

> —George W. Bush

## 🐘 Suiciders

"These people don't have tanks. They don't have ships. They hide in caves. They send suiciders out."

> —George W. Bush

## 🐘 Superpower

"We're no longer a superpower. We're a super-duper power."

> —Tom DeLay (representative from Texas, 1985–)

## 🐘 Surgeons

"Please assure me that you are all Republicans."

> —Ronald Reagan (president, 1981–1989), to surgeons at George Washington University Hospital, after being shot by John Hinckley in March 1981

## ★ Tantrums

"When White House leaders learned about my agreement . . . they proved tantrums aren't restricted to the two year–and-younger crowd."

> —Charles Grassley (senator from Iowa, 1981–), on his efforts to cut President Bush's tax-reduction package

## ★ Taxation

"No taxation without respiration."

> —Tom Feeney (representative from Florida, 2003–), voting to eliminate the estate tax

"I can't hear you, Matt."

> —Arnold Schwarzenegger, asked by Matt Lauer on the *Today* show whether he would release his tax returns

"Not over my dead body will they raise your taxes."

> —George W. Bush

"They don't make anything."

> —Mike Bloomberg (mayor of New York City,
> 2002–), on why his opponents in the 2001
> New York City mayoral election had an
> easier time releasing their income tax
> returns

"First they tax our beer, then they tax cigarettes.
Now they are going to increase the tax on gasoline.
All that's left are our women."

> —John East (senator from North Carolina,
> 1981–1986)

## Teenage Daughters

"I've got a sixteen-year-old daughter, too. She
hasn't been apprehended yet. I can't get her out
of bed."

> —John McCain (senator from Arizona,
> 1987–), on the legal difficulties facing the
> Bush twins

## 🐘 Tenants

"I don't have to accept their tenants. I was trying to convince those college students to accept my tenants. And I reject any labeling me because I happened to go to the university."

> —George W. Bush, on visiting Bob Jones University in Greenville, South Carolina

## 🐘 Tenderness

"I also understand how tender the free enterprise system is."

> —George W. Bush

## 🐘 Terrorism

"If I see someone come in that's got a diaper on his head and a fan belt wrapped around the diaper on his head, that guy needs to be pulled over."

> —John Cooksey (representative from Louisiana, 1997–2002)

"Arrest every Muslim that crosses the state line."

> —Saxby Chambliss (senator from Georgia, 2003–), suggesting an anti-terrorism strategy

"I urge the leaders in Europe and around the world to take swift, decisive action against terror groups such as Hamas, to cut off their funding, and to support—cut funding and support, as the United States has done."

> —George W. Bush (president, 2001–)

"I do have a miniature dachshund named Reggie who looks out for us."

> —Donald Rumsfeld (secretary of defense, 2001–), on his personal strategy for anti-terrorism protection

"I think Mohammed was a terrorist . . . a violent man, a man of war."

> —Jerry Falwell (founder, Moral Majority), on Islam's most revered figure. Falwell stood by his statement, but later said that "most Muslims are people of peace."

"My only regret with Timothy McVeigh is that he did not go to the *New York Times* building."

> —Ann Coulter (syndicated columnist and television commentator)

"To try to gauge just how out of touch the Democrat leadership is on the war on terror, just close your eyes and try to imagine Ted Kennedy landing that Navy jet on the deck of that aircraft carrier. I don't know about you; I certainly don't want to see Teddy Kennedy in a Navy flight suit anytime soon."

> —Tom DeLay (representative from Texas, 1985–), who did not serve in the military, on Ted Kennedy, an Army veteran

## 🐘 Thanks

"Well, thank you, I think."

> —Jesse Helms (senator from North Carolina, 1973–2002), in response to a caller on *Larry King Live* who thanked him for "everything you've done to help keep down the niggers"

## 🐘 Time

"It's about past seven in the evening here, so we're actually in different time lines."

> —George W. Bush, speaking on the phone with Gloria Macapagal Arroyo, president of the Phillipines

## 🐘 Tollbooth

"I think we need not only to eliminate the tollbooth to the middle class. I think we should knock down the toolbooth."

> —George W. Bush, during the 2000 presidential campaign

## 🐘 Robert Torricelli

"Torricelli will leave public office with just the clothes on his back, a Rolex watch and other assorted jewelry, a TV set, a couple of racks of Italian suits, some Jets tickets, a grandfather clock, and three paper sacks filled with small, unmarked bills."

> —Ann Coulter (syndicated columnist and television commentator), on New Jersey Senator Robert Torricelli, who declined to run for reelection because of ethics charges

## 🐘 Trade

"It is very important for folks to understand that when there's more trade, there's more commerce."

> —George W. Bush

### 🐘 Transparency

"You can see through that like you can [Jennifer] Lopez's dress."

> —Bob Dole (1996 presidential nominee), on Al Gore's campaign contributions

### 🐘 Trashing

"While it is important to trash the governor, it should be done in the context of regret, sadness, and balance."

> —Frank Luntz (political consultant), in a memo regarding the recall of California Governor Gray Davis

### 🐘 Treason

"Liberals have a preternatural gift for striking a position on the side of treason. You could be talking about Scrabble and they would instantly leap to the anti-American position."

> —Ann Coulter (syndicated columnist and television commentator)

"The left's anti-Americanism is intrinsic to their entire worldview. Liberals promote the rights of

Islamic fanatics for the same reason they promote the rights of adultering pornographers, abortionists, criminals, and Communists. They instinctively root for anarchy and against civilization. The inevitable logic of the liberal position is to be for treason."

—Ann Coulter

## Treasure Hunt

"It is not like a treasure hunt, where you just run around looking everywhere hoping you find something."

—Donald Rumsfeld (secretary of defense, 2001–), on the search for weapons of mass destruction in Iraq

## Tripling

"We've tripled the amount of money—I believe it's from $50 million to $195 million available."

—George W. Bush (president, 2001–)

## 🐘 Trustworthiness

"Well, I think if you say you're going to do something and don't do it, that's trustworthiness."

—George W. Bush

## 🐘 Twisting

"I think we ought to let him hang there, let him twist slowly, slowly in the wind."

—John Ehrlichman (domestic policy adviser in the Nixon administration), to Nixon White House Counsel John Dean, on acting FBI Director Patrick Gray

## 🐘 Unacceptability

"For every fatal shooting, there were roughly three nonfatal shootings. And, folks, this is unacceptable in America. It's just unacceptable. And we're going to do something about it."

—George W. Bush

## Underwear

"Change your shorts."

—Tom Ridge (secretary of Homeland Security, 2002–), telling Jay Leno what to do if a yellow alert is issued when he's in his underwear

"Boxers or briefs? Don't even think about it!"

—Colin Powell (secretary of state, 2001–), to an MTV audience

## 🐘 Unemployment

"But if you've been laid off of work, you're 100 percent unemployed, and I worry about it."

—George W. Bush

## 🐘 Uniter, not a Divider

"When it comes to sew up your chest cavity, we use stitches as opposed to opening it up. That's what that means."

> —George W. Bush, asked on the *Late Show with David Letterman* what it means to be "a uniter, not a divider"

## 🐘 University of North Carolina

"University of Negroes and Communists."

> —Jesse Helms (senator from North Carolina, 1973–2002), in 1950

## 🐘 University Politics

"University politics are vicious precisely because the stakes are so small."

> —Henry Kissinger (secretary of state, 1971–1976). Kissinger taught at Harvard University for many years.

## 🐘 Unknown Unknowns

"There are known knowns. There are things we know that we know. There are known unknowns. That is to say, there are things that we know we don't know. But there are also unknown unknowns. There are things we don't know we don't know."

> —Donald Rumsfeld (secretary of defense, 2001–)

## 🐘 Jesse Ventura

"I was a mediocre high school wrestler, and I wear a feather boa around the Senate on occasion."

> —John McCain (senator from Arizona, 1987–), asked about his similarities to Minnesota Governor Jesse Ventura

## 🐘 Vials of Tears

"Who is Terry McAuliffe kidding? If Bill Clinton were president on September 11, he'd be selling vials of tears Clinton shed that day."

> —Craig Shirley (political consultant), responding to the Democratic Party chairman's criticism of Republicans giving pictures of Bush from September 11 to political donors

## 🐘 Victoria's Secret

"I know what Victoria's Secret is. She's a slut."

> —Barbara Cubin (representative from
> Wyoming, 1995–), chatting with campaign
> donors

## 🐘 Vision

"There's a substantial amount of issues visionarily
that we're going to be discussing over the next
eighteen months."

> —Rick Perry (governor of Texas, 2000–)

"Do I have a great vision to make Louisiana the
best state in the country? I don't know."

> —Jay Blossman (2003 Louisiana
> gubernatorial candidate)

## 🐘 Vocabulary

"Spending programs are now 'investments,' taxes
are 'contributions,' and these are the same people
who say I need a dictionary?"

> —Dan Quayle (vice president, 1989–1993)

##  Vulcanization

"What I am against is quotas. I am against hard quotas, quotas they basically delineate based upon whatever. However they delineate, quotas. I think vulcanize society. So I don't know how that fits into what everybody else is saying, their relative positions, but that's my position."

—George W. Bush (president, 2001–)

## War

"With which country?"

—George W. Bush, asked by the media about going to war

"I think war is a very dangerous place."

—George W. Bush

"I've been to war. I've raised twins. If I had a choice, I'd rather go to war."

—George W. Bush, who was a member of the Texas Air National Guard and never served overseas

## 🐘 Wardrobe

"I need to work with him on his selection of shirts in hot auditoriums."

> —Trent Lott (senator from Mississippi, 1987–), on Al Gore's heavy sweating during his speech to the Florida Democratic Party

## 🐘 Washington

"One of the things I had to get used to in Washington—and still haven't—is that everybody kisses everybody else."

> —Dick Cheney (vice president, 2001–)

"It's a hell of a challenge."

> —Conrad Burns (senator from Montana, 1989–), asked by a constituent, "How can you live back there with all these niggers?"

"After two years in Washington, I miss the sincerity and genuineness of Hollywood."

> —Fred Thompson (senator from Tennessee, 1993–2002). After leaving the Senate, Thompson became a regular on *Law and Order*.

## Watergate

"We have tours on Sundays from two to four, ten dollars, no cigars."

> —Bob Dole (1996 presidential nominee), after he and his wife, Elizabeth, purchased Monica Lewinsky's condo at the Watergate Hotel, which adjoined their apartment. Prior to purchasing the apartment, Dole commented that "I walk by very fast."

## Wealth

"[Internet millionaires] who have become rich beyond their means."

> —George W. Bush, during the 2000 presidential campaign

## West Texas

"I was raised in the West. The West of Texas. It's pretty close to California. In more ways than Washington, D.C., is close to California."

> —George W. Bush

## 🐘 Whenever

"We are trying to change the 1974 Constitution, whenever that was passed."

> —Donald Ray Kennard (Louisiana state representative, 1975–2003)

## 🐘 White House

"It is white."

> —George W. Bush, asked by a British student what the White House is like

## 🐘 White People

"White people, wake up before it is too late. Do you want Negroes working beside you, your wife, and your daughters, in your mills and factories?"

> —Jesse Helms (senator from North Carolina, 1973–2002), in 1950

"[I wish you could be here in Illinois to see] all these beautiful white people."

> —Nancy Reagan (first lady, 1981–1989), on the phone to Ronald Reagan, after Illinois had been hit with a sixteen-inch snowfall

# 🐘 Women

"Bodybuilders party a lot, and once, in Gold's—the gym in Venice, California, where all the top guys train—there was a black girl who came out naked. Everyone jumped on her and took her upstairs, where we all got together."

> —Arnold Schwarzenegger (governor of California 2003–), in a 1977 *Oui* interview

"I'm not for women in any job. I don't want any of them around."

> —Richard Nixon, explaining why he nominated William Rehnquist to the Supreme Court

"Like most women, my wife thinks with her glands, not with her head."

> —Mark Hatfield (senator from Oregon, 1967–1996)

"Those are the prettiest witnesses we have had in a long time. I imagine you are all married. If not, you could be if you wanted to be."

> —Strom Thurmond (senator from South Carolina, 1955–2002), at a Senate hearing

"Women are best suited for secretarial work, decorating cakes, and counter sales, like selling lingerie."

—Larry Koon (South Carolina state representative, 1975–)

"I saw this toilet bowl. How many times do you get away with this? To take a woman, grab her upside down, and bury her face in a toilet bowl? I wanted to have something floating there. . . . The thing is, you can do it, because in the end, I didn't do it to a woman? She's a machine! We could get away with it without being crucified by who-knows-what group."

—Arnold Schwarzenegger, describing a scene in *Terminator 3*

## Work

"It's true hard work never killed anybody. But I figure, why take the chance?"

—Ronald Reagan (president, 1981–1989), in 1987

**Youth**

"Blessed are the young, for they shall inherit the national debt."

—Herbert Hoover (president, 1929–1933)